I COULD HAVE BEEN MORE WRONG

POEMS

KEVIN McCAFFREY

Illustrations by Dana DuMont

FOUR WINDS
PRESS

For Elizabeth and Aidan

Table of Poems

Country *Commedia*

for Lesleigh

You be Virgil, I'll be Dante,
then play your part so well
that even Peter Handke
would say you're doing swell.

As smooth as Jimmy Durante
reading from that *Book of Thel*,
just play Virgil to my Dante
and lead us both through Hell.

Times are tough though, I mean, aren't they?—
they've got that brimstone smell.
Vigilantes in flagrante,
we'll have such tales to tell:

how we drank up the Chianti
and into darkness fell
before, like Virgil *in avanti*,
you led this Dante out of Hell.

Soft-spoken

My father to the sick company came,
a competent manager whose voice was soft
as he issued commands in his plain
way, making sure nothing of worth was lost

in the overwhelmed processes. The men
perceived he was not your typical boss—
not a loud-mouthed dictator, backslapper,
moody narcissist, nor cheerleader

whose easy praise and exhortations pall
with each repeating. And when his words were whispered
from his grey, thin lips, men listened, enthralled,
then returned to their machines—his sprung words

still unwinding in their minds. The rise and fall
of stamps on dies, whistling belts, turning gears,
and all the other mechanical sounds
a factory sends droning out to drown

the human spirit resumed, but his thoughts,
through all the relentless noise, held their place
in the men's minds; seed-like, they put down roots
and grew, made a woodland of the brain,

saplings first, then trees, in that fecund spot,
so that each found some solace from his pain,
his mind become placid, a shaded hill.
And still, for all that, the factory failed.

My father and his men dispersed. Some went
to other towns, to other factories,
boating on economic tides; some spent
themselves in idleness; the luxury

of free time is costly—in time it sent
them to wander our town's streets, the town green,
these tired men made ghosts, in bearing listless,
near but unseen, purified by uselessness.

In time, unlike these men, whose spirits died,
the tides of commerce returned; a tidal wave
of capital crashed through our region. Why?
What will be re-exploited must first be saved,

so the factory was reutilized
and surged again with sounds of belts and lathes.
But that calm, soft-spoken foreman was gone,
replaced by me, his screaming asshole of a son.

The Brazen Sonneteer

Is there a window broken? How? Perhaps
a mad old bird, a cardinal, came crashing
through? Or is there a back door found unlatched
when it should have been securely fastened?
Is there a subtle inkling that the safety
of our home's been breached, though evidence
is slight? There is. And it changes the easy
satisfaction we take in this our residence,
our splendid home, tonight. It just feels off,
as if each chair's been sat on, each fur stroked,
and every gem handled and ogled and pawed
and then put back—until we find this note
writ in a hand round and flip and clear,
this taunting sonnet by the Brazen Sonneteer.

The Eagle

Here are the shirts the eagle has laundered
as he works to meet your stringent ideals;
he'll do his best, this chance won't be squandered—
he'll zip around your airy rooms with zeal,
cleaning, straightening, fluffing, and buffing,
vacuuming, cooking, and making the bed.
For your happiness he's always fussing—
he likes your nickname for him: "Talon Ted."
And if at odd times he emits a screech
and rips up, say, Grandma's hymnal,
some of your standards may be out of reach—
he might never make full bird colonel,
this one you think you've lured to your luxe lair,
though he just tends to go where eagles dare.

The Struggle Is Real

Smash the fascist regime all you want, dear,
but can it wait until tomorrow?
I've had some hassles and some setbacks
and that's added to the general weight of sorrow

I carry with me like a psychic sack.
Today, I'm a little tired from the weekend
since I had some trouble with the Audi.
There's a rattling from the front end.

Well, I was driving back from the city
all ready to take some time off and march today,
but there was some kind of pinging from the engine
and I've got to drive down to the Cape on Saturday

so I've got to take it to the shop
and deal with the usual unctuous perfidy
from the mechanic, plus at yoga Friday
I think I did something to my knee.

I know that this is the time to fight back—
I told my students that just last week.
We've set aside our entire syllabus.
It's time to head out to the streets.

And I'll be there, I will, in a day or two,
but would you like to go to a restaurant tonight?
There's a new Laotian place that's just opened.
We comrades should eat before we fight.

Mellow Fever

Bid the fellows to be mellow down in the hollow—
the Othellos with their jellos, do you follow
me? Hello, I'm curious yellow, may I borrow
your pomelos until tomorrow, please—
that's what they'll say I said in their tell-all, jeez,
that I bellowed like Longfellow at the Dollar Tree.

Mind

There is a mind behind your mind—
calm, cold, and dark as the vast sea—
and floating there's a fishy eye
that blinks at your complexities.

Though you may wish to swim, to dive,
into your own obscurity
to find there both the how and why
of your personality,

the descent's too deep to be described—
it's just the stuff of fantasy—
or worse, it's where truths turn to lies
amidst tidings of tranquility.

Some say it's better not to try
plumbing inner eternities—
if that is what, in fact, you'll descry,
searching for what it means to be.

Juggler

My eye fell out of its socket
then bounced back off the ground
and landed in my shirt pocket.
No one else was around

to see the unique miracle
of my bouncing eye.
You would have been hysterical,
my friend, and this is why:

I put it back into the eyehole
and it worked just fine.
It blinked. It moved. It saw. It rolled.
It connected with my mind.

Now I'm the guy with bouncing eyes.
I dribble them down the street.
Sometimes I bounce them off my thighs,
sometimes off my feet.

I'm like a juggler in point of fact.
That's how I use these orbs.
I juggle them behind my back
while hopping like a toad.

Nor do I stumble, I keep my pace
as I move gracefully.
Though my eyes aren't in my face,
they still see perfectly.

But caution, caution, little fool.
Heed my instructive words.
Do not attempt the things I do
and pull from optic nerves

your globes, for this madcap trick
has blinded many bunglers
who've ignored the obvious risks
to would-be eyeball jugglers.

These failures languish here and there,
their dreams cut down to size;
though each reviews the feat they dared,
you can't see it in their eyes.

When they sense me coming by,
they twist their necks to hear
the whizzing of my juggled eyes
as through the air they veer.

I am the cock of whom they cluck—
these pecking, clawing hens.
They could not get their eggs unstuck
and put them back again.

But when eyes fall from my sockets
they bounce back off the ground
and land in my shirt pocket,
safe, soft, moist, warm, round.

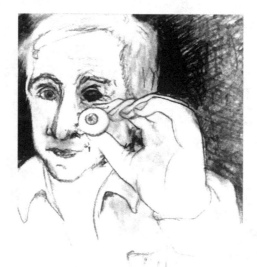

Generic

It ought to begin with a detail
or two meant to attract
astute readers' attentions
to put them well on track

to move to this next stanza
where more can be revealed—
a picture or thought should start to form
and readers might well feel

the inklings of an impact here
as things reify,
the meaning almost unveiled,
the how if not the why.

And now, brief but nearly finished,
the poem can end its flight
with readers' finer feelings set
abuzz, if it's been done just right.

My Friend Zuckerberg

He knows what I had for breakfast
and what I had for lunch,
he knows my favorite movie star—
it's more than just a hunch.

He knows my favorite TV show—
it is *The Brady Bunch*—
and my favorite soft drink—
I like Hawaiian Punch!

How does he know? How does he know?
Have I been overheard?
No, I shared everything myself
with my friend Zuckerberg.

I told him all my deep secrets,
what I dream at night,
all my slightly offbeat fantasies
of elves dressed up in tights.

I told him all my politics—
he knows just how I lean.
He knows if I am left or right
of the arithmetic mean.

How does he know? How does he know?
Have I been overheard?
No, I shared everything myself
with my friend Zuckerberg.

And not only does he know,
he guides me in my thought
by sending me special stories
that are uniquely wrought

to influence my demographic
to move towards the extreme.
He knows our will is plastic—
we're just living for a meme.

Winners Lose

In the end it's the winners who falter,
losing health or fortunes or minds
and then it's as losers they tote a toddler
up into the mountains behind

the estate and rally there quiet
for many and many a year
until the time comes and they riot
attired in really quite chic riot gear

and the child they'd rescued from death
or something boring like that
leads them to glorious conquest
of their former habitat

from which the corrupt dukes and the fabulous ladies
flee into the hilly wild
where many of them get rabies
and lose their practiced sense of style

but some of them power on through
and learn their perverted ways to mend
for they'd also carried a forsaken child who
leads them back to win in the end.

The Night Off

I told the watcher he wasn't needed,
he should spend a night on the town,
so the midnight fire blazed unheeded
and burned my precious mansion down.

No one was there to see the start—
to see how flames first crawled, then leaped
and spread, consuming every part,
from basement stone to rooftop's peak.

And when I returned from my sojourn—
I too had passed the night elsewhere—
my house was naught but timbers burned
and smoke draped acrid on the air.

And I had never felt more free
than when I grasped, my eyes tear-filled,
how this home had been my destiny—
yet I was not planning to rebuild.

Just This One Description

Someone who does not like variety,
or eschews it, that's what she is. Mention
anything regarding your anxieties
and she'll share how she lessened her tensions,
which are gone like drunkards from sobriety,
like cowards who had been needy henchmen.
The choices she once made: what clothes to wear,
where to live, or work, what meals to prepare,

what hobbies to pursue, what books to read,
what music, movies, or other interests
to satisfy her expanding needs—
this was her problem. Choosing was a test,
wasn't it, when options vied to supersede
each other, scrapping to be the fittest?
Gone now, or less urgent, are the choices
which formed a democracy of voices

within her head, each trying to appeal
to her cupidity, to gain the chance
to live through her. What's wrong with that? We feel
that markets, speech, ideas—all free—enhance
our lives; the better we choose, the more real
we are. But though the best choice might supplant
all others in the hot contest of impulse,
she could not help but feel repulsed

by so much heat. Now she's a simple soul.
What should she wear? A t-shirt and black slacks.
What's for breakfast? Jelly and a roll.
Music? What's better than a little Bach?
Books? She has chosen *For Whom the Bell Tolls*
as the one book she'll read. How about snacks?
It's salt peanuts when she has the urge,
or sometimes ice cream, an infrequent splurge.

For work, she was a seamstress with a band
in her youthful days in old Woonsocket—
a costumed group that critics often panned.
From those years she still retains a locket,
although the picture's been removed. She ran
a criminal gang next, of pickpockets
and thieves. Conflicted, she's taking a break
as a zookeeper, tending to the snakes.

Her basement apartment, what's it like?
Remarkably plain are the furnishings.
And her mode of transport? A three-speed bike
with one of those old bells whose ring-a-ling
is mild and quaint. Her favorite bird? The shrike.
Strange? She finds its sharp ways encouraging.
She too is nondescript. She too impales
experience and lets it fight and flail

before she forces it to fit her notion
of how to make life easy, worry-free,
and just as smooth as skin slicked with lotion.
Some may suspect some kind of witchery
has been at work in her, that some poison
has undermined all her complexity.
No. What's pushed her towards her plain lifestyle
is the controlled joy of self-denial.

There are no PR firms for nullity,
nor any champions for the boring.
Her quiet stand against the multiplicity
of things in our world always roaring
to be used won't impact society
at all. No new John Cage will be scoring
a theme song, moved by her self-restriction.
Of her life there's just this one description.

Rating Sorrows

Watching someone you love dying—
that's just about the worst—
but there are things almost as trying
with which this life is cursed,

such as seeing love diminish
in a lover's cold eye
and sensing that you're finished
no matter what tricks you try,

but worse—if we have to rate
the sorrow of each trial—
is seeing your love returned with hate
from the eyes of your own child.

I Could Have Been More Wrong

More wrong you said I could not be—
that I was just about as wrong
as wrong can get when it's been freed
to wander forth, clad in a thong,

through crowds of proper folk, and prim,
who only do what's decorous
and never indulge untoward whims
or do anything treacherous.

But I'm not one to genuflect—
like some ephebic cup-bearer—
before the merely incorrect,
the mild mistake, the malformed error,

for—buoyed by new stupidity—
my gaffes will climb like a King Kong
ascending to flawed apogees
to show I could have been more wrong.

Your words, become a kind of dare,
can't be undone. And though you claim
I've misconstrued, I just don't care.
An archer with the blindest aim

could never miss a target more
than I who've lashed myself, distraught,
to the mast—a mixed metaphor—
and await, thus tied, the ship's next stop—

against sharp rocks or o'er the falls
to drop, a wrong-headed sailor
who heard something like Cthulhu's call,
which beckons fools to eldritch terrors,

though it isn't fright that shapes my quest.
My ineptitude will be your curse.
Each mistake will outdo the last,
as monsoons drown a drought-caused thirst.

At each deluge you might wonder—
as Cheech was oft surprised by Chong—
as my storming screw-ups thunder,
whether I could have been more wrong.

Attention All Shoppers

The store is closing, shoppers.
Everything must go—
all the lovely products stacked on high
that with an enticing glow
under the high-hanging lights
inflame your busy appetites.

But now the enterprise is emptying—
there'll soon be nothing here.
Won't it be odd how this once bustling place
will fill with listless air
and how abruptly the unused shelves
will be as vacant as your selves?

Shoppers, attention! Heed this call
and gather what you can
from this, this sale of sales,
with acquisitive élan.
Put to a final test your buying power—
this store will close forever. In one hour.

I Spoke Too Soon

I only said that I assumed
a Dim Sum Götterdämmerung
by early afternoon to Mr. Bloom,
but that sufficed to seal our doom.

He sighed in stride to the rostrum,
muttering unspecified nostrums
that stunned—or blurred—our fun,
like Peking Duck ablaze, my son.

How inopportune for him to spume!
He cleared the room, a slurring broom,
so when time came for the news—
delivery being left to you,

a curlew perched on Bloom's preview,
who'd bird the word unsparingly—
the luncheon was already through.
What's left now of the afternoon

but fortune cookies and cold green tea?
I spoke too soon and so did he.

The Last to Go

This is the story of how she survived
at the failing organization,
survived purge after purge of those who told
the truth while she said nothing. Instead she
sat in her little office and listened
to everything the leaders said, voices
sounding self-important, as they walked through
the halls of the office building. Sometimes
a leader would poke a head in her door.
She'd smile her weak smile and say nothing.

That was the safest way. She had other
things on her mind too, things she'd never talk
about until she was good and ready.
Surely, that day would come. And it was not
as if the leaders were not good at anything.
They were excellent at talking about
how excellent they were and at pointing
fingers at those below them, or stabbing
them in the back, as if the underlings were
the reason the place was going downhill.

But she sat amidst it all, at the center
of all the frenzy, and said nothing. She
knew that when the leaders of an organization
start to go all feral then it's really time to
go inert. That way they might not rip

your arm or leg from your torso and club
you with it, just speaking figuratively
of course, though she wasn't speaking. She was
sitting and trying to avoid notice.
It seemed to be working. She went unclubbed.

But she was not just doing nothing,
although that's the way it might have looked.
She was nurturing a new self growing within
her psyche—a bolder version of who she was.
She fed it with her silence, weakness, and fright,
feeling sure that when this superior self
reached full maturity and pushed her old
self aside, then she would speak with a more
forceful voice, though even then she might not
tell the truth. How could she know what she'd do?

Creation of new selves, that's Taoist stuff,
the kind of thing you'd read about in weirdly
obscure texts found wherever weird texts
are sold. *The Secret of the Golden Flower*'s
one such otherworldly tract, describing
processes through which an adept rejects
his old self to emerge a sage. Never
had she read this book, or the like. So was
her change some unconscious phenomenon?
Maybe her transformation was a sham.

Or maybe not. Stolid pieces of prose
which march along at an unhurried pace
will burst on rare occasions into song
and a reader will say god damn, I'm glad
I'm reading this book. It's like a sunny clearing
in a fucked-up wood. Her long silences
contained such interludes. Not of song or speech,
but of deeper quiet, and at these times
she said to herself the endless bullshit
of my life's been worth it if it nurtured this.

These times of superb silence, she felt them
within herself as spans of unequaled peace,
and imagined that, fed by the brightness
of her mind, a translucent flower grew
in the red mud of her chest. Within that plant
there grew a tiny replica, doll-sized
at first, of herself. It would grow large
in time, growing into her body like
molten metal fills a mold. Did it work?
All I know is she kept her job.

She survived even as the company
foundered. Firings, lay-offs, budget cuts,
strategic plans, administrators shipped
in by the boatload and then let go—none
of this made any difference. Nor did
the logos, the new product lines, the bold
strategies. The place had lost its punch,
but could not grasp it. So one day her run
did end. The place did close. But whoever
it was she'd become, she was the last to go.

Gently Failing

Your insight into your insides is failing
but at what rate is to be determined
by outside forces when they have a mind to,
all of them relaxing into the gentlest failure
this world will ever know. They say relax
into it and you do, joining the slackening
throng. And you've got an angel by your side
enhancing your purchasing power,
so this endeavor goes smoothly. You don't
have to foam at the mouth at the
picnic anymore to get your way.
You don't have to do anything
except listen to the records they put on
when they want you to forget
there's nothing left to do.

The Nought Kitchen

She works with nothingness to
drive the world mad, making it
blasé and sad. She's a cook too in
the kitchen out by the glacier
where she cooks nothing special
for her mom and her dad. What
she does there's nothing to
whether she does it or not. She
doesn't say much either although
she's a polyglot. Some days she
stirs an empty pot and ladles
nothing into bowls. There's not
much to it; maybe it's food for the
soul.

Do You Watch Clouds?

There are worse ways to spend your time
than looking at the clouds,
and you don't have to be attuned
to anything to see these clods

of fluff for the sweet time-wasters
they are. Just let your soft thoughts float
with them if you want. In Worcester
I watched clouds join into a fleet

and anchor yesterday, stirring not
at all despite a breeze. Dullards
I deemed them. How was it they'd stopped?
Don't clouds follow natural laws?

Apparently not. Last night too
they tarried, just languishing there—
maybe they had nowhere to go
or maybe they weren't of good cheer,

though this morning they moved on,
dissipating as they sailed east.
Likely they'll be gone by Boston;
cloud watchers there will be displeased,

but they need not make totems
of displeasure   these trifles pass.
Old hands gain a certain wisdom—
clear skies are never made to last.

Mother

Mother, oh Mother, why
are you "othering" me?
I know we don't share
quite the same ancestry.

Father was a barber—
he came from Seville,
and you are a Tartar
from over the hill.

You two have your differences,
I know that is true,
but it's hurtful to hate me
for not being like you.

So let's barter, you Tartar,
oh what shall I trade?
For your loving embrace
I'll give you a haircut and shave.

Robot Spies Watching
Elves Watch a Fish

It seemed like the elves knew just what to do
after they'd caught the big fish,
which flipped and flopped now in the oblong pool
they'd cut into the rock beneath the cliff.
Relaxed, they'd spend whole summer afternoons
in moods reflective, more or less transfixed
by how light and shadow cavorted

on the sheer wall and by the distorted
shimmers the fish's movements painted on
that canvas with a twisting brush of light.
This is the scene we robots chanced upon
in those bellicose days when we were spies,
two green machines on a scouting mission
who watched in secret from the heights
and pondered how and why these elves had caught the fish
and carried it live to their basalt dish.

Our Patter

When you, the Walter Pater of patter,
contest my claim that the world gets flatter
as more step onto it with their clown feet
and stomp like fat men ambling to a feast,
then I must stop our talk awhile, love,
to glance at you with cool reproof
and that puts a stumble in our gambol,
a hitch into our ramble. The fable
stops and there is nothing left to say
except you like your latte made with soy
more than with milk, the milk of the cow,
the milk of that old cow that steals the show
and whose most heavy hooves
compact our barnyard earth like God's own truths.

Best Seller

This whorish tome is eager for your eyes,
unfolds before your curiosity,
spreading her white leaves like fevered thighs.
When she calls, you accept . . . excitedly.
Excitedly you enter, claim your prize,
to use outmoded terminology.
But soon, dear reader, your ardor spent,
you toss the book aside, only a few pages bent.

Lone Lemming's Lament

All the lemmings left this evening
to go leap off a cliff
and left me here with my feelings—
my old spirits need a lift.

I'll admit that I'm dejected.
Who wants to be left behind?
What'd I do to be rejected?
I've got jumping on my mind.

I thought I'd done what was required
and struck the proper tone,
but maybe I was uninspired;
I'll have to plummet on my own.

Cue the chorus, start them singing
with moans, laments, and shrieks—
myself I will soon be flinging;
I don't want to be unique.

Goodbye freedom, goodbye self-rule—
autonomy makes me groan.
Sometimes doing what others do
means you have to leap alone.

Counting for Nothing

I've come from the land of Nothing Matters
here to the city of Nothing Works
where I hope to climb the broken ladder
to join a company of inept clerks

who count until they can't remember
what number it was they counted last,
counting on each finger, on each member,
until the future becomes the past,

and when end becomes beginning
then the count must start again,
and no one cares that this spinning
always returns to this refrain:

I've come from the land of Nothing Matters
here to the city of Nothing Works
where I hope to climb the broken ladder
to join a company of inept clerks.

Lies Are Drawn to Truth

Lies are drawn to truth, some say,
like opposites attract,
like two-faced consorts to a god,
dishonesty to fact.

You've seen it in your own life—
the things you once thought true
have wilted, haven't they, one by one
like flowers tritely do?

Your loves, your dreams, your firmament—
ideas of who you are—
the truths you thought self-evident
were imploding stars.

Citizens of Oblivion

Did you hear it on the television,
or read it in the *Times*?
Did you see your leaders assert it
with confidence sublime?

Did you see questioning doubters
disparaged or ignored?
(If this great nation were a ship
we'd toss them overboard!)

Then if you found it was untrue,
weren't you dissatisfied,
since living now the way we do,
we've learned to love our lies?

Veracity had a good long run
till it rotted at its roots—
now we're citizens of Oblivion.
Lives are better without truth.

Festival Song

We're going to have a festival,
I've grown another testicle—
where there were two there now are three.

The evidence is incontestable,
with three warm eggs my nest is full,
though it's all a mystery to me—

how did two become a threesome
and cause this expansion in my scrotum?
Am I the first in all of history

to see something so odd
as a multiplying seed pod?
Where there were two there now are three!

Oh, it would take an Honoré de Balzac
to celebrate my nutsac
for he would write so expansively

about how dear old Mother Nature
has invented a new creature.
I'm so glad it happens to be me.

Rumination

Our parents were two white people the color
of foam. Mother was bright, father was duller
in tone. In truth, you could say mother was white
as a bone and that father was darker, like wheat
or limestone, though his hue could change with the angle
of the sun and skew towards a purple
or plum. Meanwhile, we, the two children,
when young, had a pinkish cast to our skin.

Like tongues we were colored, sister and brother,
or like roses bred—not without some bother,
one supposes—by gardeners who eschew reds
in larger doses in their flower beds.
But, you know, sis, pink days aren't meant to last.
Time passes and, like our parents, we've blanched.

Outrage

There is a town called Outrage—
everyone's angry there,
always feeling disparaged,
and ready with a glare

for all those who have wronged them—
there've been so many wrongs—
and each vies to be the victim
aggrieved most of all the throng.

To wail about one's suffering,
that is a gift most prized,
and it's a wondrous song they sing
who past wrongs rhapsodize.

Pity then those hapless sinners
who've rarely been ill-used,
those who once were deemed the winners
and never were abused,

how they yearn now to be chastened,
though it's somewhat strange—
despite so much self-debasing
nothing ever seems to change.

Yet no one dares to turn the page
on practices futile,
for citizens of Outrage
prefer the taste of bile.

Youth

Perhaps what I did was offensive—
that didn't serve as a brake—
young, my ignorance extensive,
inclined to make mistakes,

I drove down our town's main street
pretending to be blind.
It's a feat I would not repeat
now, but it still comes to mind

when I indulge in reverie:
how I tried to use sound
as well as instinct and memory
to transit through the town.

I'd made it half a mile, I'd guess,
before disaster struck—
a scream soon led to a last breath.
We'd both run out of luck,

that much was more than obvious,
though I didn't dare to glimpse,
and I have stayed oblivious,
my eyes shut ever since.

Festive Dinner

Hurry and do nothing—
　　there's nothing to do,
though you'll disappoint all
　　who, depending on you,

have dreamt such great dreams
　　of such shapes and hues
that whatever might happen
　　they'll never come true.

So let them call you the key,
　　the top gear, the oil, the glue—
they just need someone to blame
　　when things finally fall through

and come crashing down
　　or spill like a stew
to cover the tablecloth
　　in steaming goo,

while your little brother plays
　　the didgeridoo
someone gave him for Christmas,
　　which they now rue.

Huge Deliberation

If I could hug a Huguenot,
oh, if I had that chance,
would I do it or would I not
with hugging arms advance?

For I once hugged an ocelot,
it happened at a dance,
though most details I have forgot,
he looked like Bruno Ganz.

Not everyone's a Lancelot,
with stunning looks enhanced,
but aren't most of us worth a shot
when it comes to romance?

That's excluding mean ol' Pol Pot—
he is not worth a glance—
before hugging him I would rot
like some green cheese in France.

Gripping so tight that out pops snot—
at that I'd look askance.
I'll put no death hugs in this plot,
no hugging à outrance.

So, if I could hug a Huguenot—
say I was in a trance—
would I do it or would I not?
I think I would perchance.

A Resuscitative Recitative

Choking throughout the episode—
let's chalk that up to what?
Before you was a motherlode
of gemstones, gold, and rock.

Your destination was achieved—
you'd tunneled through the crust
of earth, and all the time you'd breathed
your air pumped through nickel ducts.

You'd breathed it in in splendid gulps
and whistled as you worked
with drill and dynamite and pumps.
Your dusty lips were pursed.

And then a final hammer tap—
there was the trophy room.
That cavern had pulled out all the stops!
Jewels twinkled in the gloom.

And that was when the air gave out—
the system gasped and sighed.
Goals of joining health and wealth
seemed somewhat misaligned.

You huffed, you choked for lack of air.
You were down too far to run.
And then you heard an aria
of whistlings, throbs, and hums.

You sensed it was the sound of death—
a sound which never soothes—
until you felt that first fresh gust
in your throat and nose.

It was like a soft-voiced art song
or melody of reeds—
that sighing sound as the air resumed
its hushed recitative.

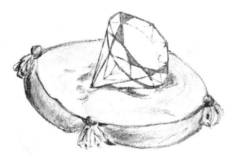

Blakelock

She also thought up the raffle prizes,
including Blakelock's painting of Black Flag
in which pogoing Indians and fairies
surround the punk band while blazing bonfires
cast lurid hell-light across the canvas.
Oh, to have been young that night in Kansas
so long ago, to have danced there with the tired naiads
as they crumbled towards another dawn—
that would have been a moment heaven-sent,
but would not have topped what we'll achieve,
sisters, at our oleaginous event.

His Last Board Meeting

Labhraíonn an gealt.

I would like to make a motion,
knowing it will be voted down.
Given the situation
and the troubles that surround

this too optimistic enterprise
which we love to celebrate,
I move we look with clearer eyes
so as to recalibrate

our chances of succeeding,
which diminish by the day.
Though we aren't good at heeding
those whose dismal views dismay,

I raise a lone voice to caution—
fully aware that truth's taboo—
since failure is our only option
and there's nothing we can do,

let's call a stop, close up shop,
bring this meeting to an end—
there's no way more useless talk
can reverse our downward trend.

Being and Time

On your *Dasein* she has designs—
she wants to steal your being.
And while she beckons with a smile,
you really must be fleeing.

Where will you go, where will you go
when the world's expanse is endless?
If you will go authentically,
you must toss aside your compass.

Adrift amidst swamp and cliff,
forlorn peak and canyon,
you'll leave behind your sense of time.
You'll live with true abandon.

You'll perch and lurch and curse and search
through stunted larch and alder
for one clear space in the thorny waste
with a stone there like an altar.

There will be no priest or marriage feast
or choir soft and soothing,
with only night to attend the rite
when you join yourself to nothing.

You will be nothing in the world—
yet you will have such power;
from nothing flows each passing day,
to nothing dies each hour.

Enchanting wife, bountiful life—
these are what you will be leaving.
Alone with just time and fate,
you'll comprehend your being.

You've fled, you've fled a downy bed
and a life of warmth and order
to find your soul and join with death
in a land that has no borders.

Here Is the Document You Requested

Here is the document you requested.
The information has been well digested.

It delivers its deliverables
with the strength of fifty enwheeled gerbils.

It is grounded in accepted practice,
yet questions and redefines the status

quo, thus it emits an aura or glow,
so those who don't heed it encounter woes

aplenty. A most puissant document,
built upon a foundation of cement,

figurative cement, by which one means
it does not support insubstantial themes.

Its arguments—or points—lie as beavers lay logs out
when they dam streams, pushing their wet snouts

against the bark, although they use tooth
more than snout, one guesses. It's also true

this document is more deeply conceived
than beavers' usual work, for beneath

the logjam, in the moist, the clammy cavern,
the boggy darkness, the beaver tavern

where beavers' eager industry reposes,
when, spent, it like this summation closes,

or ends—there the rest, made for rodents,
is unlike what this sage document foments.

This document makes one act, energizes.
It also comes in many fonts and sizes.

Apprentice

Long hours, arduous and taxing,
learning every nuance
of a trade so damnably vexing
that if I but had the sense

I would run off to something else,
to easier success
where achievement comes with ringing bells
and minions nodding "yes,"

I would pursue another trade,
but thereby hangs the tale—
my making will be to be unmade,
when I master how to fail.

Glider

There was a man who'd learned to fly
though not so very well—
he never really reached the sky
and he often fell.

Through our nowhere streets he'd glide
a few feet off the ground,
until with something he'd collide
and come tumbling down.

Naturally we were envious
of this human pigeon—
and, even more insidious,
envy became derision.

That airborne man we'd bait and hound—
what insults we'd sling—
and when we'd brought him to the ground
we'd laugh at his clipped wings.

If all can't fly then no one should,
that was our conviction—
ours was a no-fly neighborhood
and better for the restriction.

Karl Marx, Lord of the Leprechauns

Some things were carried from the area,
some were pushed or rolled. The biggest things were dragged,
which put an end to the hysteria
so they were steady enough to unbag

the implements they needed to perfect
the space, make it radiantly pristine,
with each square inch laboriously swept,
then polished, then misted, then rewiped clean.

Who did this work? It was that echelon
of fairy folk who once upset our plans.
Oh, what a change in the wee leprechauns,
now that Karl Marx is fully in command.

It was "Leprechauns of the world unite,
you've naught to lose but chains and habits old."
He made those fairies communists. That's right!
They've nationalized all their pots of gold.

They were the wiliest, weirdest miscreants—
than bats, badgers, or ferrets more perverse—
prone to nab a man's coins from out his pants,
or steal his child, or lay a heathen curse

upon his soul to damn his once bright eyes.
Unseen, barely sensed, this unseemly band,
until that day they got organized
and the fairy's friend, Karl Marx, took command.

They do not call him leader, citizen,
or other term from the red lexicon,
no, it's "Lord" the wee folk quaintly deem him—
Karl Marx, Lord of the Leprechauns.

Anger

In angry times the angry win
Pyrrhic victories,
since those championing chagrin
sing threnodies unwittingly.

To a Sexbot

You look like someone I once knew
but without all the boo-hoo-hoo.

Shanty

We're not dauntless explorers, no,
we already know the route—
we've hidden our failings far below
so as to seem resolute,

we love to shout we're sailors bold—
we're riders of the storm—
but actually, if truth be told,
we revel in the norm!

Our trade wind is hypocrisy—
we're the self-deceiving sort—
we've set sail for mediocrity,
our most familiar port.

Our ship is called Ambition
but that's a misnomer sure,
since our fundamental mission's
to arrive at where we were.

I'm Not Lethargic

You only learn to sit like a horse sits
after you learn to lay
your hairy back on the carport
floor with a patience that evades

explanation, though
it might pass for standard barnyard apathy
if looked at in the right way,
or maybe just stone-cold lethargy.

Hey! I'm not lethargic—
that's what a donkey brays—
though I do like to rest up
and wait for those better days.

Better than what, old donkey?
Better than the day before,
so I'd better get myself good and ready
by resting on the floor.

Back to the Grind

It's hard to make a telepathic baby.
I know because we've tried at least three times.
It's more than just an idiosyncratic hobby.
We've worked on it so much we've grown weary.
Our skin has turned a morbid shade of lime.
It's hard to make a telepathic baby.

You have to mix the actual with the maybe—
combine science with magic, blood with wine.
It's more than just an idiosyncratic hobby,
since success would end all our worldly worries.
We'd have a guide—a pure, all-seeing mind,

but it's hard to make a telepathic baby—
it's a process that we just can't hurry
and we need to cross some ethical lines,
so it's more than just an idiosyncratic hobby
as anyone can see quite clearly,
but we've got to get back to the grind.

A Proposed Law Banning Necrophilia

When I am dead, my body spent
and lying cold, waiting for the grave,
will I still have a chance at love?
Not if the state legislature has its way.

And if my long life's companion
should wish one last fond test
of my dwindling desirability,
will she be denied more than a chaste kiss?

If it's true that death will free us,
clear away all thoughts and fears that vex,
who are these prissy representatives
to keep the future dead from sex?

Put me before your assembly,
you living, breathing makers of the law.
I'll tell you your lifetime of rules
will not constrain me when I'm gone.

Put me before your Great Court,
hear me aver with my last breath—
my last physical act will be my retort,
my body is still mine in death.

As memory through time devolves
to less than memorabilia,
no living law will dissolve
the hope of necrophilia.

Funny Love

Funny how my arm flew off
at our first greeting.
Wasn't it then that you remarked
that human life is fleeting?

Gashes appeared across my face;
my blood flowed strangely too,
since it spurted from my cheeks
into my Mulligatawny soup.

Funny too how my leg blew off
and how you laughed and tossed
it spinning across that restaurant.
I hardly felt the loss.

Next my tongue, my nose, my ears,
and then one of my eyes.
That's how our first date went for me—
while you sipped your chai—

until I was just a limbless torso
and head propped in a chair.
I was such a silly spectacle,
but love was in the air.

What kind of love was it
that filled that atmosphere?
The kind that blows a man apart,
yet leaves his soul so pure

that he can see desire itself
and break its funny codes,
for our bodies so obscure love
true lovers must explode.

Nightfall on the Shore

for Peter Dudensing

You and your fellow Zennists
play a cerebral game of tennis—
not in thrall to net or ball,
you always beat the dentists.

After the match is finished,
you lunch on leeks and spinach
within the walls of your dining hall;
the repast is delicious.

Then, if portents are auspicious,
you sail out towards Saquish—
with nary a squall to cast a pall,
your spirit is replenished.

But though the day is cherished,
sunny pleasures must diminish—
nor prayer nor call can forestall
twilight's periodic dimness.

So let night win this scrimmage—
let darkness bathe the fishes—
nightfall will enthrall one and all
like a witch who knows her business.

And know there is no redress
once day begins its egress.
Your hammer, maul, even your awl—
each one of them is useless.

So for you South Shore Zennists,
lct this knowledge be your penance.
Time may crawl, but the warrant's scrawled—
no sunny day is endless.

New Muse in Town

"The most thought-provoking thing in our thought-provoking time is that we are still not thinking." —Martin Heidegger

Last night, enraged, you said my life was sad.
Then you downed a drink and went, half-cocked,
upstairs to bed. I didn't follow you, glad—
if that's the word—we'd have a chance to talk
when morning came, which it has, the launch pad
to yet another day—hurrah!—that rocks,
or will, mutable love, when you arise
to beats, and moods, as yet unprettified.

And if I did not pass the night in sleep,
but crept, a shade, the shadowed house,
waiting for some sign—sigh or floorboard's creak—
that you were soon to be up and about,
I am not overtired. Matters aren't that bleak.
There are many things I want to recount
in full detail as we sip our day's first beers.
Yes, I want to discuss all my ideas

with you, my former life companion's closest
friend . . . and some questions too about the terror
contorting the expression of our "hostess
with the mostest": did we act in error
when we knocked her off her throne? It's grotesque
how just we two were the lone pallbearers

at a funeral which involved no one
but "we who've learned the power of a gun

to mend dysfunctional situations" . . .
like your tired habit of sleeping through the day
when we have got to man our battle stations
and map out the new roles we'll have to play—
philosophers now in cogitation—
presenting ideas in inspired array—
theorizing realms of thought and being.
Perhaps I'll fire a few shots through the ceiling

to help you escape your slumber, and if
that does not help you face the day head-on
I don't know what I'll do. Ineffective
approaches to our problems tend to spawn
new sets of problems—that's always the risk.
One moment you're in the game, then you're gone.
One moment you're resting in a friend's room,
the next you're waking with a sense of doom

and wondering what idiot is firing
a gun in the house, fucking up the floor.
That idiot is me, patience expiring.
I was thinking deeply, but I got bored.
All my scheming grows so uninspiring—
it's like a symphony built on one chord.
Such dull music needs your orchestrations,
coy bombast, and thoughtless provocations.

How does one thought push another aside
and rise to dominate a mental space—
how does one urge undam, then surf the tide
of mental energies? All night I faced
my thoughts, seeing some fail and some abide,
rising, in their own time, to extirpate
their kin, and hoped that you, persuasive friend,
would answer me: where does such thinking end?

Land Acknowledgment

Hey Native Peoples everywhere,
we're living on your land—
it was stolen years ago
by the always bad White Man,

but do we aim to give it back?
Gosh, that is not the plan.
Instead we wrote this pathetic statement
so you'll better understand

how sad we are, how bad we are,
how perfidiously bland.
Were you expecting something more?
Hypocrisy's our brand.

Gunnar

Disliking Gunnar is easy—
you fear he'll go berserk at work.
Now this Viking makes you queasy:
is that an ax he wields or a smirk?

No longer will you share the flagon
of this bursar who sailed from afar
in a boat sleek as a mechanized dolphin;
he also drives a Swedish sportscar.

Though you came, virgin, to his temple—
this Wotan with a clipped accent—
and he made life seem so splendidly simple,
now your infatuation is spent.

You felt something once, a real feeling,
but—hold on!—is that really true?
His videos were revealing—
he did things we just do not do.

You tried cajoling, then pleading,
you even tried music therapy,
forced him to sing, his voice wheezing—
my god, but he's a tuneless canary!

You once longed for his long boat,
vowed you'd sail through oceans to prove
you loved him though he was icily remote.
Now you want these memories removed.

Let him guard gold from troll and dragon,
let him do those things bursars do,
you won't again share his mock Nordic flagon—
your liking for this Viking is through.

Pink Secession

The red forest keeps itself covert;
it's wrapped in a black fog.
To the main road we must revert,
the way of the macaw's claw.

The way of the claw is the standard,
the stand-up-and-be-counted way,
and each of us pink-cheeked bastards
has little to say but "nay!"

That's the way it's going to go
now that the forest is hid.
We march on tippy tip toes.
We are in a snit.

For pink dreams are like cloudforms
that take on newish shapes,
wobbling to defy norms
or billowing like faded drapes

on windows looking down on the forest
(when it can be seen). Think,
before it's left up to the florist,
how everyone hollers for pink.

In the pink of our life we shake a fist
at both the red and the white.
We will be pink exceptionalists
until the two unite.

So show us red trees, vines, rills
bathing in white moonlight.
We'll remain aloof until
forest and moon unite.

Look Out Below

I was the last one to fall from the sky,
trains of tailwinds trailing,
with few thoughts left to occupy
my falling or my flailing.

Updrafts caught me unawares—
how they sent me sailing—
and all I had done to prepare
was unavailing.

Yes, winds took me for that while—
westerlies prevailing—
rocked me, rocked me, as a child
by a mother wailing

for a world that comes on too fast—
what use is all our railing
when this falling does not last
beyond one last exhaling?

Procrastinator

Now that I haven't done nearly everything
and there's almost nothing left not to do,
maybe I'll make a list of some new projects
which I won't get to later on this afternoon.

Do you ever get that woeful feeling
when far too little's left to be half done
and you say, "Is my work finally unfinished?
Should I all but plan a sojourn in the sun?"

And you might call me a procrastinator,
you might scream that as you walk out the door,
but don't expect me to say we're over,
for me there's joy in uncompleted chores.

No, it's not a joke, it's a lifestyle—
it's more than just a maddening caprice.
Procrastination is my vocation—
my life's an unfinished masterpiece.

Holyoke Range

None would call you majestic—
you're not that way at all—
boasting no summits splendid
nor any waterfalls,

but your serpentine undulations,
running along for miles,
prompt, if not exhilaration,
a familiar smile

in those who savor local treasures
down to the last detail
and who've learned to take their pleasures
on a smaller scale.

The Missing Page

One page too few in the *Collected Tu Fu*,
the librarian laughed when I told her,
and the more she said there was nothing to do,
the more that I grew colder,

so I threw the verses, with many curses,
at the unhelpful help-desk occupant—
though it was one of my many near misses,
I did break the arm off a succulent.

Lawn Parties

Hidden meanings visit us—
they've taken human forms—
they're moving in odd patterns
out on our front lawn.

The neighborhood has gathered—
an ever-swelling throng—
to catch a wisp of wisdom
before the troupe is gone.

You say it looks like modern dance—
I say more like chi gong,
but whatever it is they're telling us,
we'll likely get it wrong.

Some of the troupe have tambourines,
some of them have drums,
some of them have banjos
they vigorously strum.

And some of them are singing out
while others remain mum—
from what they say it's not quite clear
where they're coming from.

But most of us will follow them—
yes, after them we'll run—
to dance a dance of hidden meanings
on someone else's lawn.

Reformed Hunters Seeking Praise

When gloom plus doom the whole ravine
has filled and prospects bleak
have undermined those who, unseen
for the most part, seek

to live simple lives as critters,
then what can come along
at the right time, like Kurt Schwitters,
to help them sing a song

that's new? To the extent that they
can sing, I mean, which is,
except for the birds, not the way
they, these animals, give

voice to their furry feelings.
Therefore on every morrow
are we seeking, while they're reeling,
ways to assuage their sorrow.

But that's just us, reformed hunters,
who now aim to play roles—
by giving woodland creatures succor—
that others will extol.

Questionable Choices

Lives run parallel to our lives—
the lives we should have led—
and how often do we ponder
how things might have gone instead,

if we had just done differently
what we did years ago?
It's not like it's a mystery,
the problem is we know

how each day could be so wonderful
that with delight we'd squeal—
if not for a few questionable choices
we'd be living the ideal.

Can You?

Your day starts in an empty room
with a bewildering machine,
and no one tells you what to do,
or what, in fact, success might mean.

And after an indecisive hour
you try the switches and the knobs—
you think you have turned on the power
since the thing starts to hum and throb

as if some vacuum tubes are heating
and hidden gears are being spun,
though your excitement soon proves fleeting—
futility has just begun.

But it's not a miscalculation
to spend your hours on such a chore.
Compared to many occupations,
this one doesn't seem like such a bore.

So tell yourself these words of wisdom
as the day chews up your essence,
repeat them till you numb your tongue—
can you slow hope's evanescence?

My Sinecure

It's years of work and I've attained
a precious sinecure.
In return for minor pains
and slights, my lifestyle's assured

and though I have to work for fools
I cannot be deterred.
Don't make waves—that's my one rule;
let not the pot be stirred.

I used to be a lion bold,
you should have heard me grrr,
but I'm a cat now that I'm old—
I roll and loll and purr.

Set me aside with comments smooth—
your damned disdain is clear—
just so as you do not remove
my precious sinecure.

Activity! activity!
Let action be your spur,
for that is the proclivity
of you young managers.

But leave me useless on the bench—
the game seems such a blur!—
for I'd be just a monkey wrench
dropped in your spinning gears.

I know why *this* caged bird sings,
why flight holds no allure.
My mind is on just one thing,
my precious sinecure.

Bagatelle

for Keith M., our Adonis

Relaxing in a shady bower,
that's a good feeling, yes,
as is dashing through an April shower
while devoid of dress,

but it is March and thus too harsh
to let swing the apparatus
as we prance by fen, by marsh,
in pursuit of sweet afflatus.

Grandpa's Babysittin'

Years ago I was involved
in an act of procreation—
and in time a child arrived
after a period of gestation.

That child grew and grew and grew
and then became a mother—
she had a child, in fact two,
a sister and a brother—

so if you're looking for the cause
of why today fun is forbidden—
let's chalk it up to karmic laws—
grandpa's babysittin'.

Minor Irritations

Here's to minor irritations,
vexatious interludes,
to the passing consternations
that on my day intrude.

Let them rain down in torrents
or come each out of the blue,
these testers of my tolerance,
upsetters of my mood.

I know how life can pack a wallop—
how it can devastate—
run over things at quite a gallop,
even as I murmur "wait."

So give me these little setbacks—
let them come frequently—
I'll take a million such attacks
over any single tragedy.

Fight of Their Lives

As two fighters in a late round—
absolutely spent—
yearn somehow less for victory
than for the fight to end

and for a moment's privacy,
each in his dressing room,
to contemplate the fragility
of bodies shaped by wounds,

so this once bickering old couple
no longer waste their breath
on a mutual repugnance
that can only end in death.

No One We Know

Successful, oh-so-successful,
in all she did and said—
and at the same time oh-so-humble,
so that all those whom she led

uttered praises without ending
for all she had achieved—
in short, it was so mind-bending
it could not be believed.

To many, yes, she was godlike,
so powerful, so calm,
solving problems both left and right
with rectitude and charm.

And all was quiet elegance—
her home, her stylish clothing—
a life marked by abundance,
all fueled by her self-loathing.

Capitulation

I'm so sorry—that's what I'll vow,
that's what I'll protest,
my voice so much calmer now
than when I wasn't at my best

just an hour or so ago
when we were arguing.
About what? Oh, I don't know—
some inconsequential thing.

Yes, I was wrong, which I'll admit
to let the situation heal—
though secretly—a hypocrite—
it's not really how I feel.

It's easier saying I'm not right
than to endure the pain
of another long drawn-out fight,
since you won't do the same.

Blaming the Help

Bridget, Bridget, where's my hair?
I see that it's no longer there.
Do you think it was the au pair
who took it to her attic lair?

If she's a witch, as you claim,
perhaps she's set my hair aflame
in some dark rite—obscene, arcane—
while the moon is on the wane?

Perhaps she snipped it while we slept
and did not hear her muffled step—
and when my stunning locks were clipped
quite quietly away she slipped

to braid with it a magic doll
to conjure with, since my downfall
is what she seeks and that's not all—
what will go next, now that I'm bald?

Wrong Turn over Mars

"What is the right term for 'making
a right turn' in your Martian tongue?"
I queried our pilot, a zealot
who'd started out life on a heap

of dung, but the rocket was thrusting
and I fell back to trusting
he knew his way round the planet
from which he had come. My approach

was mistaken; the craft started
quaking, and I began to lose
my customary composure,
   or equilibrium.
Then my story turns gory,

an insane allegory involving
   a spaceship,
a timeslip, a wig-flip, and
a trigger-happy earthling
with a broken ray gun.

A ray gun is trusty, effective,
when not unexpectedly defective;
it will cut through anything like a
really bad mood. And, just like
   invectives

and frenetic gestures, they're standard
    fashion accessories
in this gone neighborhood. So any
slow-walking spacer in need of
a pacer, who's glacially placid

when he's not in the mood,
will tell you to your visor,
howsoever you vie, sir,
don't try to cold-cock your driver

if you can't access level four
stun, or you may find yourself
swimming, uselessly skimming
towards that unfortunate endpoint
    we hail as the sun.

That Hairy Harem

When the storm stops you'll leave in sheep shoes.
You'll wend your way through the suburbs.
You'll walk like a man with nothing to lose
who's adjusted his amp to full reverb.
Of course they're distorted, since your meanings are loose
and your nerves swerve across to tomorrow, but
there's old black magic in forgetting to choose—
you can float like the wind through wind tunnels
or creep the rooms of my father's house
like a desperate man, shepherd, or criminal.
There may have been reasons galore
for breaking in, though no one is there to hear them—
no, not even that rain-soaked Zsa Zsa Gabor
you left with the harem of airmen.

Asphalt Gong

My boys thought up the asphalt gong,
then your boys went and made it wrong.

It was supposed to sound real nice,
like mud thudding onto dirty ice,

or like a toad hopping down the road
just before a bomb explodes.

But it sounds more like a tire's squeal—
for me that sound holds no appeal.

Does it for you? Well they're your kin,
the ones you fished from a trash bin,

the ones who went and made it wrong,
my boys' idea, the asphalt gong.

Tomorrow

Hey, have you ever at the fall of dusk
walked a new-built, gated community,
felt the coolness of the grass? So plush,
the feelings there of trust, of unity.

The houses are all upper-middle class. The streets
interweave according to cogent plans.
The fresh-laid pavement submits to your step;
the place symbolizes the transformed man.

And the parks where youngsters play merrily,
the saplings planted at set intervals—
they point, one might say, almost warily
to fresh, unfolding miracles.

So our packing begins tonight. Soon we'll
begin the move to our new locale,
and if we have been somewhat unfulfilled
up until this point—nondescript vales

overgrown with underbrush, sweating vines—
those square landscapes will set us straight. God,
how our future neighbors get their yard work done!
To turn souls grassy they can lay the sod

and make a self as calm as perfect lawns.
Soon we'll be trim-cut too, no longer crude;
our shrubs will be shaped, we'll hum suburban tunes
as we take our place in that neighborhood

where just-so Colonials parade back-to-back—
they have such understated rectitude,
such gravitas. There's nothing wack
about those shacks. Tomorrow is the day we move.

Danger Makes Three

Sisters they are not, though they could well be.
They do not share familial ties. Their looks
have nothing in common. As for esprit,
enthusiasm marks the one, while rebuked
and weirdly vague the other seems . . . unworldly
too, though it's hard to say what might have spooked
her. Bottom line: the woman's reclusive.
Why? The evidence is inconclusive.

Yet outward differences sometimes cloak
similarities within. The allure
of danger motivates them both. As yokes
are central to the egg, the startling whirr,
the fierce, adrenalized uprush that stokes
the heart's engine centers who they are. Pure
excitement is what these strivers thrive on,
like taking the last chopper out of Saigon—

in short, that's the feeling these women seek,
but they quest for kicks through different modes.
One's path is overt. The other's is discreet.
The first obtains sensory overload
through courting peril. She savors peak
experiences—diving in abodes
of sharks, piranhas, snakes, and octopi,
or skulking round haunted sarcophagi.

She's a spelunker too, descending alone
into the cold earth's innermost recesses,
and a ski jumper who, chilled to the bone,
exults in airborne flips. Such excesses
delight her. So too does hunting with stones
and a slingshot, leaving rotting carcasses
of grizzlies, lions, boars, and ocelots
behind, though these trips tend to cost a lot,

so she can go hunting but once a year.
Her friend, with whom she shares a house, eschews
all this heroic stuff. She's quirkier.
She'll creep at night into her boss's office to
put a live snake into his desk drawer,
or break into a vacant ranch house through
a jimmied window or French doors to scrawl
obscure dictates, crayoned on bedroom walls.

What does she write? Just nonsense rhymes mostly.
She's playful in her criminality,
remaining out of sight, lurking, ghostly,
reshaping her humdrum banality
with harmless trickery. She guards closely
these private acts. That's her mentality,
though she tells her housemate of her forays,
since they both respect each other's tastes.

They love to share their stories when there's time
to make a cup of tea and smoke a joint.
In living room or den their voices chime
together, intertwine, emphasize points.
They laugh out loud when details are sublime
or twisted. With oily praise they anoint
themselves heroes, avatars of aplomb—
two friends joined with danger, a threesome.

After

To counter Sirens' singing,
you bind yourself to the mast,
but now that the bark is sinking,
your knots hold too damn fast.

It's odd how the best solutions
can lead to something worse—
how hope can gleam deceivingly
and prayers become a curse.

When it comes to what will come next,
that can be oh-so-plain to see—
it's what will happen after that
can spell calamity.

Acknowledgments

I would like to acknowledge the invaluable assistance of many people who have read through these poems or offered insights, suggestions, and support, including Lesleigh Brisson, Aidan McCaffrey, Elizabeth Murphy, Chris Benfey, Michelle Ducharme, Elizabeth Lloyd-Kimbrel, Bill Newlin, Owen Andrews, John MacKenna, Gerald Costello, and Jim Hartley, as well as Tony Lee and other members of the Naked Running Club. The poem "My Friend Zuckerberg" appeared first in *The Texas Tribune*.

About the Author

Kevin McCaffrey has published a novel, *Nightmare Therapy*, and a 2014 volume of poetry, *Laughing Cult*. His poems have appeared in *Exquisite Corpse*, the *Trib Talk* section of the *The Texas Tribune*, and *The Writer's Almanac*—all of which became defunct not long after his work appeared. He lives in South Hadley, Massachusetts.

About the Illustrator

Dana DuMont is an artist, illustrator, and educator based in Richmond, Virginia. She exhibits and teaches regionally, collaborates on a broad range of creative projects, and is often found communing with dogs, ecoprinting, or repurposing thrift store media.